ZERO DYNASTY

The Behavioral Correctiveness in Children
Versus Western Biblical Principals of
the Sparing of the Rod Syndrome

ANEB JAH RASTA SENSAS-UTCHA NEFER I

 www.trafford.com
North America & international
toll-free: 1 888 232 4444 (USA & Canada)
fax: 812 355 4082

KING NARMER

King Narmer was an ancient Egyptian King during the Early Dynastic Period as well as a early unifier of Upper and Lower Egypt. Narmer has been considered founder of the First Dynasty. Within this, appeared the Protodynastic Period {DYNASTY O}. You see, within those two periods there were observative measures as they relate to divisive nations / regions that were within the entire entity of the Egypt Era.

Narmer unified the natives of both Upper and Lower Egypt. In addition;

King Ka, which means to 'embrace'. In this, Ka within the Kamitic spiritual tradition is known as the Sahu Division. The sahu division is termed as the {fool, with gullable behavioral patterns of insecurity}.

This is due to his / her being in constant usage of the{it] lower faculties of the brain {stem}. The brain stem in known to the hippocampus throughout western medicine, psychiatry and social sciences. In addition: th [reptillian] {according to the Kamitic Philosophy.

This includes Sphere numbers 7-8-9 and the manefestation of magnetic fields that are within the Sephirotic System of Ten Divine Names according to the Hebraic Cabalistic Traditions. Therefore; many scholars have spoken and have written that there is factual evidence of Egyptian settlements in Israel during the Protodynastic Period.

During this period there then existed various distinctive patterns of trade. Trade where the so-called Hebrew Israelites claimed their doctrine of Judaism. This is also where Canaan existed along with trading routes as well the trading of exports along the marketing and solicitation of brutal lines of sodomy, lewdness, homosexualities and prostitutional slavery got their hidden and unrevealed names.

Note: one must understand, that the base word in Sephirotic is Seph / Ceph which leads to [Cephalagia = Head—Brain Trauma] also leads to the ancient Greek word, Encephalomlopathy. Encephalopathy means brain disorder. When you add another base word to it, such as Myelo— you find out that it equates to Myelooencephalopathy. This is when you become induced other physiological and neurological disorders. These disorders include the following: Immunological diseases and and disorders; They include neurotic, psychotic and venereal diseases of the Sexually Transmitted Disease Type.

Therefore: Cepazolin is an antibiotic, anti-STD and anti-viril infection medicine. In this, this particular medication has been prescribed for patients that have faced near death experiences resulting from scientifical and investigative studies that have included as patterns cohesive with the provision of inmunizational methods. Those methods include providing undocumented injections of transgenetic organism of pathogenetic effects unto and within nearly every living organism.

Moving right along, Narmer made his presence felt and recognized in Canaan through politicalisms and war. Due to the establishment of new kings in lower Egypt. The majority of them having received rank through religious and spiritual mockery of deceitfulness and decensions. They intermingled with the following cultures: Arabians—Cretians and Romans. This is when vile invasions occurred.

Therefore: In this book, ZERO—PRE AND PROTODYNASRTIC PERIODS OF The Behavioral Correctiveness in Children verses Western Principals of Sparing The Rod Sysdrome = You, the reader will gain greater insights within the knowledge and understandings of racial and cultural barriers that were manipulated and transformed by the western uncivilization for millions of reason. This is generational and has been coupled by individuals, leaders, politicians and greedy and shrewed business owners. By those who have falsified the rights, greatness and of wisdon of Kamit through the undermindment and abolishment of its divinity and greatness. This holds true today. The civilization of Kamit lived through self-descipline. This includes strict methods and holistic approaches {health} through dietary measures from views of spiritual cultivation that has been sanctioned today by overpopulating those who are oppositional and defiant towards the Afrocentric spiritual point of view(s)

The views include the healing methods of voodoo {vundun}, meditation and divinational healing. These traditions were brought to the United States of America and Carib Nations of {Yoruba} Nigeria and North West African. The origins were from Predynastic Egypt,

ProtoDynastic Egypt, Kamit, Canaan and The Nile Civilization of Indus Kush. This is when European nations fellowshipped (gathered) and constructed the Atlantic Slave Trade. In this, they conquered Morocco—the Moors—of Spain and developed the Middle Passage and Triangular Trade. African children were defiled by the means of rape, molested tortured and maimed by their captivators. Also, one must understand that marriages, homes, mothers, fathers, sons and daughters were separated by the caucasian. The ancestry of Japhat continued to shape and mold the Black Man, King and his Mate (Queen) by the use of force with sex farms. This is where individuals were auctioned and forced to perform lewd sexual acts. Kings and Queens were sodomized within areas and psychiatric diagnosis of Fetishistic Disorder, Paraphilic Disorders and other dominant methods of lewdness.

They were beaten with those objects and maimed in front of their families (clan)—(tribemens / women). Those irrational acts of torture and violence were used as patterns towards the evolvement, cultural dominance and revolution of the white man. They used revolutionizing behavioral modifying methods to satisfy their arousals by behavioral shaping in order of achieving and maintaining the powers of decivilization and dehumanizing in order of regulating divisive economic strategies in order of creating an overpopulated prison— juvenile system.

This system of economic development was formed as a quest to remove the male from his kingdom—head of his household, make his mate—wife into a harlot / prostitute. This has lead many into transforming themselves into the customs of the western uncivilization. Modernity is forever becoming a far more lazy, effiminate and vagabonding culture within the Black community. This is far more worse within the environment of those with narcissistic and delusional patterns of psychiatric dysfunction. These reside as caucasian within small caucasian communities. In addition: this is beastiality, prostitution, transvestism and opiod—herion addictions.

As mentioned in Metu Neter Vol. 4 pg. 201—By Ra Un Nefer Amen I—

"Laziness is the number one cause of an individuals failure to applly his / her self. This is due to the segregative thinking that occurs and is released within the Cerebellum and Cerebral Cortex when the two haven't been spiritually cultivated. You see: those patterns of brain function also governs the spirit—characteristic through imitation, manipulation and schematic methods of imposition. Therefore; the modern African American and African has adopted the ways of the western behavior as to the evolution of the enhancement of increased stress, unhealthy diet and instability. This is due to various forms of escapism and scapegoating through the survival methods that are imposed by the reptillian {hippocampus} portion of the brain.

Drug abuse was introduced to Black soldiesr within all of American's wars. Diseases were then passed on stemming from The Greek, Arab, Roman, Christian and Jews through the invasians and separatism that occurred by emperial grand wizards of the kkk, police officers, sheriff, political figures and ministers within the Islamic Mosque, Coptic Church and unto western Christianity through the Jim Crow era.

African Americans were in constant battles against the struggles and challanges of receiving beatings and lynchings etc. Therefore; today, we use the term {spare the rod on a child}. You see, this is the modern form of Willie Lynch. This has been handed down as{GENERATIONALCURSES} within the Black commnunity. See: I-Ching Hexagrams Biting Through and The Well as the two has confirmed these important truths issues of truth.

Therefore; they must be examined throughly. In addition: this is a result: they are children of a curse as written in II Peter 2. Children rebel by becoming delusional and filled with uncontrolled issues of lacking self-esteem, having anxiety disorders, anger management issues and disobedience of Romans chapter 1. Indeed: this is also due to the post-traumatic mental state his or her victimization of {neglection} [by his— her siblings—parents—circle of friends}. These are triggering devices of abuse, neglect due to enticing and seductive patterns of rewarding those who are spoiled and do not deserve reward.

This is a holistic use of escapism. Therefore; laziness will impede ones progression towards the achievement of his / her divinity. This is to say, one's dietary intake of psychotropics, nicotine, caffeine, sugars, starches, sweets along with VARIOUS forms of animal and pharmaceutical supplements will eventually damage an individuals functioning level of the following; SNS, ANS AND CNS.

In this: this is to say the above listed are toxins. Toxins are poisonous chemical compounds that are then created into solids as a capsule and or tablet. Truly, they are hazardous and are keys factors in causinf cancerous viruses. These also have tendencies to cause the following; heart diseases, edema, angina, anemia, high cholosterol, liver cirrosis individuals often have IBD within the rectum,—anus. Yes, the digestive system is interuppted due to constipation which leads which is a result of strains within the abdomen and it interior abdominal muscles. Note; the lungs and kidneys at often-times lose their proper form of circulation as a result of carbon monixide that should be released.

Howerver, it is not released proplery due to the addictions with regards the listed toxins. Brain tumors, swellings and deteriation of portions of the brain also occur due to certain portions of the brain not receiving the proper intake and circulation of oxygen and blood within their proper valves.

Moving right along, the life-force of Geb according to the Kamitic Tradition, if not properly cultivated can become a detrimental downward spiral towards an individuals physical vehicle and psychological state. Therefore, Geb is the retainer of all of the metaphysical forces and resources of the universal and earthly anatomy within man's divinity. Geb is also the physician of man's divinity. Geb comprehension level can be positive and or negative. This is due to one's ability of maintaining men ab throughout stressful situations—trials and tribulations. Indeed: his / her desires and wants versus it's needs of earthly resources in order of maintaining longevity {lifespan}. On the otherhand, while on planet earth this can and will eventually turn to spoils as a result of the overindulgence of and within the lower divisions of the spirit of The Metu Neter and I-Chings shaping factors.

In this, is the spirit of one's divinity is only governed by more than the eleven laws of the Paut Neteru! This is to say, This is much more of an abyss due to the omnipotential factors of an indivuduals divinity of prelife, present life and afterlives. Therefore; man must know, understand and constantly re-affirm his / her true form of divinity.

This divinity is known and one's true self and the identification of being one with all.

In the Christian Bible it says that God is no respector of persons.

However; it also says to love your enemies. You see: this is allegorical by the means of hypocrisy and delusional within the framework of western theology, philosophy and psychiatry. This is just the opposite within the Kamitic Tradition. In the Kamitic Tradition, Amen and Ausar are recognized as being one with all as a divine being. Whereas: we are all created within the image og God! Finally, too, it is also known and recognized that this incorporates working on ones divinity by the a rigorous ritualistic exorcising format of tranforming the powers that are cultured and cultivated within.

You see, manifesting and cultivating true and positive divinity that incorporating and enhancing spiritual maturity allows individuals to manefest the powers of understanding the infinite powers of electromagnetic forces of negativity. This is to say, you'll be able to comprehend and demolish all pathological forms of negative toxins that include the following: Physiological, spiritual and psychological.

Indeed: they are electromagnetic forms of energies with hidden agendas that are willing to remove your divinity from the face of the universe. This is done by the manipulation of you lower being.

CHAPTER 1

THE PSYCHOLOGICAL DYSF UNCTIONS IN NEWBORNS AND CHILDREN

In neurology, clinical medicine and various forms of psychiatry there are intensive approaches and procedures that occur in efforts to seek cures within the entire neurological system. The neurological consists of the entire physiological INFRASTRUCTURE of the anatomy of mammals as well as all creatures that have the capacity of intaking energies of oxygen and exhaling carbon monoxide. Also, the so-called origin of western neurology has its between the sixteenth and 19th centuries.

Therefore, if anyone knows any form of world history as well as religion and spiritualy, they will understand the crucialness of trade, slavery and the quest of individuals seeking creative forms of wealth.

This is to say. The creation of wealth at the hands of servitude, indenturedness and a variety of unique methods of experimentational researching modules as they relate to vile efforts of racial exclusion.

Exclusion to the point of physical, spiritual and psychiatrical torturing through the betraying of the lowly.

In this, there were many experimentational approaches that disheartened and seperated races, people and families from themselves. Although, this story can trace back billions of years, I will not even go there. You see, constant changes within the developmental infrastructure of cultural customs and egotistic values have ignited negative behavioral patterns in adults and has had an affect upon children throughout the world. This systemic infection has spread like carcinogens. Most importantly, it has been a terminal disease. This terminal disease is that of egoism, hatred by imitating instincts of the animal nature. This is the eldest nature with all things that breathes life.

This is knowledge as to being aware of the spreading of neurological disease within the entire world. However, this has made a major transformationunto thewestern civilization. Note: that within the Zero Dynasty and prior to and now within the Kamitic Traditions and its uses of PreDynastic teaching of Ancient Egypt and Indus Kush—it is known as the Reptillian.

You see, egoism has its linkage within the all cultures after the intermingling of Japhat. European nations and its inhabitants have always existed as forms of uncivilized, unstable institutions of greed, lewdness and lustful behavioral patterns. That is to say: those men and women lived within caves, were cannabilistic and omnivorous while eathing the flesh of wild animals. This activity is far more worse today.

Moreover; animals whom were eaten by the majority of the earlier inhabitants on earth—ate each other—. Those who survived were survived by the legacy of eating of each other throughout their entire existence on planet earth. This too is a legacy that has its linkage within and through the re-evolvement within all institutional forms of of slavery, mercantilism and industrialization.

This is by the means and the creation along with the development of junk foods, sugars, dyes, artificial flavoring, artificial colorting and fast foods that eventually leads one towards addictions, aggresstions, cardiovascular diseases, cancerous epidemics, greed, lies and various forms of grandiousity. This is to say that these foods have been processed and has been given the seal of approval—Rites of Rassage as to having and fulfilling the dreams of the disinfranchising slaver.

You see, the non-western mind, the godly, just, rightcheous and holistic divine being of the past.

The past, present and future along the racial lines the Zero Dynasty,

Kamit, Indus Kush and Canaan were and will always be mimicked, mocked and ridiculed by the uncilivlized, uneducated and immature individual who realms within the sahu—khaibet divisions of the 11 laws of Maat and The Paut Neteru.

In this: The Zoroastrianism Religion of ancient Islam wjich was reconstructed within the (Urdo Language) was never mentioned thart its origin was from ancient Kamit and Canaan along with the regions of Indus Cush. Then again re-established within the cultures of Persia and the Arabia's after the two conquered Kamit, Canaan and Kush. This is to say that it's religion was derived from ancient Kamitic, Canaanite and Hindi scriptures.

This has been a concept by the generations of and after Shem. They are know as the shemites—or semites. Also, note that Imam A'la Maudud, was born in India. While his parents were of decendants of Turkistan— Central Asia. Maudud reconstructed the Holy Quran to satisfy his own intrigue. He also opposed women who had identified themselves as independant—heads of state. To found themselves" his is to say "those who found themselves". Whereas; he was too an Orthoxox Sunni muslim who opposed the Ahmadyah Movement as he was also aware of the great teachings of African spirituality. However: he had never given homage or recognition. Therefore, he died of kidney and heart failures. This is contrary to his teaching of vitality and spirituality. Had he applied his knowledge of Kamit, Canaan and Indus Kush he might have live a more healthy life.

You see, this is written in my third book—{The Schizophrenic Black Church of The Jihad} as well as on pages 30-31 within Ra Un Nefer Amen's book "An Afrocentric Guide to a Spiritual Union. This is also where it is mentioned that there has been rebellion by the white man as he promoted continued forms of anti-propaganda to his fellow whites who were (Semites and Eropeans") when they came down from Eurasia in to Mesopotamia around 2500 BC, he ran into serious problems with his woman.

Therefore; the Greco-Roman along with the Arabs concepts of western religious thought was created to form unhealthy relationships with women by using religion as the main form of shaping humanity and most importantly the entire race and culture of the African and African American male. This includes the masculation of women. In this, there was the creation of slavery through methods of sexual abuse, drug addiction, kidnappings, lynchings, castration, maiming, torture and maniacle methods of religious psychiatry.

You see, this has been confirmed as western man has rigorously cultivated his lower being—the animal part of the brain—in order to satisfy and fulfill his lustful appetite and ego with regards to pleasure.

Pleasure by the means of the so-called Imam, orthodox priest and clergymen of Christianity, Judaism and Islam. In this, they themselves know where the truth has come from. they know that it was stolen from Ancient Kamit, Indus Kush and Canaan. This is where they have failed to give recognition to its Kamitic and eastern ties.

How then can we have Kegema if lies have been generational. How then can there be peace within the realm of Godman / Godwoman if your spiritual leader such as Sayyid Abdul A'la Maududi are a part of the legacy of Jihad. Therefore, where is the kegema if there is no justice for children, the poor and women. Emotionality is animalistic in nature. Unknowingly, you gain the behavioral pattern of yor spiritual leader. If true—you live love. If you are loyal to a fictitious and rebellious leader, you then become irrational and animalistic in nature as a replica of your spiritual leader, doctor, counselor, teacher, parent, guardian and or political leader.

Have you been Shamanized by forms of the Shang Religion by the leader of your congregation, school psychologist, psychiatrist, peer, parent, sibling—clan members within your [circle of friends]? Note: your circle of friends can and will eventually harm you or kill your dreams and visions. In addition and yet, it is indeed by those who have practiced Shamanisim or have used their practice to receive unlawful gains of wealt, prosperity and esteem. In addition; do you have hidden agendas or hidden enemies? Hendrik Clarke said "your teacher is your enemy"!

Therefore: choose whom you shall serve. Kegema is therefore; K'un is the form of receptivity within the I-Ching. It also serves as northern and southern hemispheres of the brain and the universe. These are spiritual forms of physic energies of static electromagnetic life-forces.

In the Kamitic tradition it serves as Nekhebet and Uatchet.

Therefore; children are you more receptive to your authority figures higher or lower being. Meaning, the upper level of the Paut Neteru or the Animalistic Level of the Paut Neteru. Or have you been prematurly introduced and seduced into western thought through Judea-

Christendom or one of the variants of Islam and Judaism. Therefore; this is through the hypocrisy as well as false teachings of the immature, uneducated and dangerous individuals. Their karma ignites negative forms of animalistic and demonizing spirits of delusion.

They are unhappy, often depressed, lonely, gossippers of prostitution, harlotry, fashion and effiminism. They and are plagued with veneral diseases along with internal diseases of the para-cardial index as well as diseases of the digestive, urinary and circulartory areas of their anatomy.

CHAPTER 2

PSYCHOLOGICAL DYSFUNCTIONS AND THEIR PATHOLOGY ONWARD AND WITHIN CHILDREN

Pathology is the nature of study that gives reference regarding the notion that any that can produce a disease, infection and virus is known as a pathogen. In this Transgenic Organisms are capable of producing all of the aforementioned categories. In addition, ovaries can be easily affected as it will have an affect upon the fetus. This is when the fetus infected through transmissional responses molecular stimuli is manipulated while being receptive {receiving} DNA strands from spermatogonium.

Therefore: a postsynaptic neuron is a receptor that allows electrical impulses to be transmitted by the releasing of chemical neurotransmittors. Chemical neurotransmitters are amino acids, forms of glutamate, aspartate, norepinephrine, dopamine, serotonin, histamine, epinephrine {adrenaline}.

Therefore; the hormone epinephrine is extracted from animal tissues and created into medicinal producing chemicals. On the otherhand, adrenaline is a hormone that is secreted by the adrenal glands in order of increasing stress and blood circulation, breathing and carbohydrated metabolisms by preparing muscles for exertion.

You see, the role of the reptillian—hippocampus is not always negative as it relates to the conditions and behavioral patterns of learning along with its processes as many scholars have mentioned.

However; it can have negative impacts as underlying causes of neurodegenerative diseases and disorders.

Truly, receptors are proteins that reside on membranes of the postsynaptic neuron. As previously mentioned: This is a receptor that produces, induces and deduces electrical stimulated responses of impulsivity.

Impulsivity as it relates to the neuropathology of behavior through DNA Methylation and Interbreeding of the modern humans as well as those of the following prehistoric classes; Neanderthal and Denisova Hominin Genome. This will be discussed later.

Therefore: GABA Neurotransmitter(s)—Gamma Amino Butyric Acid— is and are the chief neurotransmittors of the mammalian central nervous system. Whereas; it induces and inhances neural excitabilit{ies} and adrenalin within the entire nervous system as it also regulates body mass and muscle tone.

So, as to say, Genomic Imprinting as well as Transgenic Organisms play important role within every aspect of a species humanity. This includes the physiological, neurological and biological social sciences that are greatly accepted by those who are considered as devalued.

Therefore: there is a misconception of the usage of stimuli that includes receptivity. The misconception is by and through the disharmonizing of the will and the spirit of the {TRANSGRESSOR}. These patterns and linked unto the children as they are passed on geneticly from the universal laws unto the parent [genetic imprinting] and finally unto the ovary—fetus of unborn through intercession.

These then become extreme forms of mental disorder within the society realm as it relates to the following; circle of friends, religion institution, politics, family and institutions of education throughout the world. This is also a representation of the failure to adhere truthfully to the more than 11 laws governing the spirit.

Negative behavioral patterns also occur within the realms of ancestry. Whereas; towards present and futuristic events of manipulation. Therefore; the initiators {devils} lives are continual through the manipulation of the lower faculties of the spirit [unto others]—[the spiritually immature]—this is accomplished (secretely) in order to maintain their acclaimation and authority over others.

Slavery and generational curses are patterns on manipulation. Whereas; today the will is often confused with one's purpose of divinity and level of achievements by sources outside one's self / indwelling intelligence. This is the result of Judeao Christendom, the rise of islam and Greco-Roman origins of philosophy, medicine, science, mathematics and religion.

Therefore: genetics of the entire human race has been spoiled and are in shambles today by the lack of understanding, lack of devotion and lack of knowledge regarding the True God. Every culture identifies with their fallacious god while on the otherhand; World cultures as well as culture in America and African nations of today has continually conformed to the mythological religious systems.

This is to say: its style of clothing, foods, healing, music and social / family customs etc. Surah 22:5 We please to remain in the wombs till an appointed time, then We bring forth babies, that you may maintain maturity. And of you he is caused to die, and of you who is part back to the worse part of life. Whereas: this is slightly similar to Psalm 121:4. In

Psalm 121:4 says the following: he who watches over Israel never sleeps nor slumbers.

This is a unique form of circumstance and development. Whereas; everyone is a divine being within the image and supreme likeness of God.

However: there is only one God of which everyone is within the likeness thereof. Therefore, western civilization, culture and religious fanatics have materialized and manipulated the supreme creator through obsessions of its own forms of satisfaction / self-gratification and materialistic materialisms of environmentalism.

Environmentalism deals with neglective and obsessions through the improper use of the will. These are negative aspects of the faculties of 6-7-8-and 9.

Not to mention the fact that every God Man / Woman is the invention and plan of Ptah. Whereas; his / her divinity and being are governed through the principals of Geb-Malkuth. Therefore; it is said that you govern your own world. As every living being realms upon it.

You see, if God never sleeps nor slumbers and you are in the image of God—you will eventually lose your realms of peace, rest, life-force and most importantly, your men ab. Also, within world religious and cultural affairs as well as the semitic philosophy their belief systems are based only on believing and faith—deeds etc.

This will not fly. That to say there is no proof of God dealing with their internal—spiritual growth and development. Otherwise, there are no and would have been no past or current holy-wars within the Islamic,

Christian and Jewish Sects. This goes way beyond the Holy Bible and The Holy Quran.

These are generational issues of mental illness that occurs not only through forms of mental distress.

These are occurances that have, can and will occur resulting from ancestry. Ancestry through the negative forms the attempted forms of extermination of certain classes of cultures and the individuals within those particular races at the hands of the so-called privileged.

If I must say. Allow me! There are House-Niggas and privileged white men who have dwelled upon the peacefully divine and reconstructed their divine customs into cultures within a culture of disorder in order of fulfilling their khaibet behavioral patterns. In turn, they devised a scheme of religion, medicine and psychiatry for wealth.

Therefore; This behavior has slowly dissolved and imprisoned the true nature of culture throughout the entire world. This is a carcinogen of molecular pathogens that have been excreted from the breaths and wombs of the Biblical and Quranic scholars for thousands of years after their invasion and theivery of the Zero Dynasty unto the Ancient Kamitic Tradition.

Not to to mention: Genesis chapter 36 says the Horites were of Canaan. Whereas; Esau took his wives from the daughters of Canaan and Ishmael. Ishmael was an Arab. Arabs are semitic. Whereas; Esau's wives were into (intermingled) marriage in order to conquer the divinity, wealth and land of ancient Kamit—Indus Kush.

Earlier, in Genesis 25—Esau sold his birthright for some stew {lentils}. Whereas; Jacob soon became Israel according to Genesis chapter 32. Now, let's observe the health laws of Geb. You see, lentils are vegan. That's what Esau gave to Jacob.

However; throughout the conquests of Kamit / Canaan the Africans—throughout slave transporting unto the America's as well as in modernity, individuals were and are either unaware of or ignor the observance of the 11 laws of the Paut Neteru. This is where is where the following are vital towards the achievement of one's divinity.

A: Drinking a healthy amount water daily. B. Getting at least 6 hours of sleep nightly. C. Exercising daily. This leads to the higher aspects of greater form of divinity, health, vitality and nutritional spiritual awakings according to the Uatcha—uatch-nar the utcha !

The Bible is allegorical. Allegorical's definition is defined as fictional and metaphorical. It is opinionated.

However, the Metu Neter Oracle by Ra Un Nefer Amen are great books. His vision contains forms of God.

However: Omnipotence is Gods. The only true God.

Therefore; this goes far beyond his superior works. His works allow the God Man / Woman to shape his—her negative behavioral conditions and patterns through meditation and yogic expression.

Those are steps towards divinity. Whereas: he mentions—expresses this himself within his own writings {the 11 Laws of God—page 84. "It cannot be shown through daily giving thanks, prayers, meditations, rituals reading scriptures and so-on, these are preparatory practices for struggle".

This has been revealed unto mankind unlike Joseph's prophecy according to the LDS. Therefore: who are you. Are you are divine being. Are you looking outside of your inner being in order of fulfilling / entertaining your animal nature through unbalanced scenerios of granduer.

This is to say "REPTILLIA". This is where the DSM comes in handy by experts in the field of psychiatry.

Are you suicidal. Wisdom cannot and should not be handed over unto the spiritually immature and uneducated. They'll use this to manipulate the lower being of others. As they are babes in the field of the oracle. Therefore; it is unsafe to have wisdom if you aren't living beyond the 11 Laws of Maat—The Paut Neteru.

You see, polarization is two different forms of divisive opinions and or patterns of beliefs. Therefore; there are conflicts of opinions. However, it shouldn't be for the causes of impartiality. Impartiality is of God. Therefore, leave the details to The True God.

Are you one with all. Are you one with The True God. Are you one with your enemies However, impartiality—like other words become allegorical unto the point of the scheming intellectual of Eshu. I mentioned this earlier. Are yo with me.

The negative aspects of Eshu deals with the following: pathogens and diseases: They are {lungs-bronchial tubes and COPD, CNS, PNS, ANS, Irritability, Intestinal tract disorders, speech impediments, motor and sensory neuron—nerve dysfunctions}.

These occur through pathogens of Nekhebet and Uatchet in the negativeforms of electromagnetic life- forces that disable and or hinders the progression of one's endeavors throughout life. Let's go back to what happened to Easau as the treachery of King Saul. King Saul—was Apostle Paul—of Tarsus of the Asian Minor.

King Saul seduced and deceived the witch doctor of Endor who summoned Samuels spirit in 1 Samuel 28.

You figure the rest out for yourselves. Whereas: ancient Endor was and is Canaan—now Syria!

Moving right along: Ezekiel 37:9 is when Ezekiel was told to breath from the four winds that slain must live.

That was the Shepsu. The Four winds represent the metaphysical powers and forces that are known as the universal laws of the spirit (Metu Neter) and as written in the book of Colossions Chapter 4 and Galatians.

CHAPTER 3

In addition; elemental powers are weather conditions that are manipulated forces of nuclei—through inertia.

Therefore; conditions are forms of slavery. What are you conditioned unto. Conditions are indulging features of energy that then is welcomed through portions of your brain. Stimuli is invoked by you or someone other that your divine being unknowingly.

Back to my point! This differs from Paul's dealings with the witch in Endor. Whereas; he disguised himself as someone else. He was with two women. Also, note the fact that the verse "I will put my breath into you and you will come to life", is also in the Book of Genesis during the so-called creation of Judaism and Cristianity. In addition; the Holy Quran says that "we made you from a clot of blood, germ and dust". It also says that we will what we want in your womb. this is written in the {THE PILGRIMAGE]!

However: in the Predynastic era of Egypt {Ptah}—deals with creation, structure, order, planing, life, death, resurrection—rebirth and judging the dead and the living. Seker also is a representation of bones.

Therefore; the cycle of life never dies. It is a continuing process. Whereas; everyone has things within them that must die and of must be born through Auset and the Utcha of Heru!

Ancestors guide you through God. Life-forces interact with the totality of one's being, soul and spirit. Dry Bones in Ezekiel can also represent, ligaments, tendens, joints, muscles and connective tissues.

Therefore, western education, religion, philosophy and medicine has done the people a dis-service. It has failed humanity.

Now, emotional polarization is the yin and yang, Ausar and Auset as well as the Tehuti and Maat. A duality of knowledge, concepts and ideas that brings forth and mulitiplies all things. Ausar! They've—the slavers— have come together to dissolve the entire world civilization, culture of spiritual divinity and awareness by everything that I have mentioned so far.

On the otherhand; depolarizartion is a form of stimuli, nuclei that either gives, increases and or decreases electric current (charge— energy) through the integration or segregation of stimuli. This includes psychiatric conditions of the pns, cns and or ans. You see; we have been distabalized by subliminal forces that are outside of our being. Once we begin to recognize that our anatomical development is shared with the laws that are governing factors of the universe that are shaping factors of our mental, physiological and divinity—our receptivity level will then become the major determining factor that will make us one with all.

Most importantly, one with God!

Motor and speech dervelopment deals with the cerebellum and Eshu. Therefore, the cerebral cortex, limbic system and cerebrum have millions of functions within each of them. There are muscles within each of them that manipulate stimuli processess of circulation. In this, oxygen—energy—current and electricity within nutrient energy of the universe— universal laws are congruent with man's human anatomy through the periodic elements. These elements are considered by most as vitamins and or supplements that we lack or over-indulge.

You see, we are born with the animal spirit that is within the khaibet spirit. Realization of divinity is a blessing as to becoming and being Ausar. The effects of stress within our brains, the pre-frontal cortex becomes damaged due to poor diet and or overexposure [mercury] {low-lives]—[living the nature / lifestyle of the negative aspects of Sebek. For, they attack your divinity and lower being as did the whiteman, Semite and Arab in bringing us to the America's / intermingling through trade.

Emotions diminish the spirit. You must live your readings. Therefore; here is a quote from Shechem Ur Shechem, "You have to know your culture to defend it!

Therefore—The Shang of Asia and the Ancient—Zero Dynasty, Ancient Kamit, Ancient China and Indus Kush have be the sole providers of historically great wisdom.

Chapter 4

THE ROLE OF ANCESTRY TRUE SPIRITUALITY AND NEUROLOGY OF THE NEWBORN

Are you Archaic? Have you read J.A. Rogers' Nature Knows No Color Line. Therefore: there have been tests that have compared and included the following species within their own origin: The Neanderthal—Netherlander—Portuguese—Spaniard and Denisova hominin genome with those of six modern humans: This has been an expression of the modern derogatory practices of intermingling. The majority of people throughout the world face the delusional disorder of {Ancestor Deficit Disorder} —

A: Kung of South Africa—The Kalahari Desert—Namibia and Angola

B: Nigerians—Portuguese—Hispanic—Frence and and Dutch

C: Frenchmen—see Nigeria—

D: Papau—New Guinea—Bougainville Island {BUKA} Germany French Explorer Bougainville—a French Explorer—Aboriginines of Austrailia

E: Han—Chineese—Consists of all underlying cultures within this (a-g) section. Religious practices include: Bhuddism—Taoism—Islam—Hinduism—Christianity various Egyptian Philosophies

F: Melanesians of Papau and New Guinea

G: Bougainville Islander—See (D)

The above listed origin of people have within the DNA Methylation.

Therefore; when DNA Methylation occurs—it represses gene transcription. Repress means to tame or subdue something by force through genetic imprinting means to genes to behave in a manner that is specific to the parent of origin. This [parent] does not mean maternal or paternal—it specificly means undlying cause of an ailment, disorder or syndrome. This leads to the modern language as it relates to "Transgenetic Organisms".

A Transgenetic Organism is an organism which has been modified injected material from another species. This is through genetic modification by the insertion of DNA into an embryo with the assistance of a virus, a plasmid or a gene gun. The embryo becomes like what has been injected within it.

So what then is true spirituality. Spiritualities aim is to reclaim and reshape ones divinity by constant truths of holitic measures and methods that includes self-atoning rites towards achieving, attaining and consistently maintaining divinity. John 17:14 I santify myself that you too might be santified.

Therefore: too—can everyone santify themselves as did Jesus. Who then are you. Whereas; the spirit is and can be a powerful manipulative and sublime of force through DNA Methylation! Also, Ancestral Deficit Disorder is a powerful form of struggling forces that are within the majority of individuals who have any form of health deficiency, this is to say, whether it happens to be psychological, neurological, physiological and or immunological.

These forms of deficiencies can coincide withone another. There are various defects that affects the ovaries—through fetal alcohol syndrome. The unborn is affected and infected various forms of neonatal disorders that can also have affects upon and within the adrenal glands. In this, this disorders causes epileptic seizures along with glomerulocystic disease. {Mammilian Kidney} Nephronophthisis is a genetic disease that causes liver—kidney damage, occipital and retina disorders. These genetic disorders occur in the fetus. This worsens as the fetus becomes an infant, becomes a child and eventually grows into an adult.

Now, the mammilian and hippocampus portions of the brain as the two relate to one another by cohesively become mates. Whereas: their functions are within of the Neurotransmitters GABA—Gamma Amino Butyric Acid deals with emotional behaviors of the adrenal glands that can include traumatic forms of psychotic features. Those features include inappropriate situations of granduer, maniacial aggressions with patterns of compulsional delusion.

This is to say: The entire world has The Ancestor Deficit Disorder. This is due to everyone having been caught up within the realms of delusion, allusion and compulsion.

Chapter 5

K'un
HEXAGRAM #2
THE RECEPTIVE

In the I-Ching, K'un is a representation an individuals uses and conditional patterns of expression due to their ignorances as this relates to their often usage of the so-called [FREE-WILL].

Also, this is an unexcusable use of stimuli—as is the [Do a Deed concept through the origins The Islamic Religion. This as well includes—THE I am only human Excuse within the realms of those involved within the Origins of The Roman Catholic Church, LDS and of the Judeao-Christendom Religions that includes that of The Priest—Martin Luther.]

Therefore: in neurology as previously mentioned—it seeks to find the underlying cause of causes of major neurological symptoms, deficiencies and disorders of the entire nervous system. this also includes neurodegererative diseases, disorders and dysfunctions.

Moving right along, neurotransmission allows receptors to approach the adrenal gland and produce stimulated forms of impulsivities within realms of neuropathological behavioral patterns. This is truly from within the human ancestry of The Archaics—{Neanderthals and Denisovans}.

Who were the mates of Adam and Eve's sons, Cain, Abel and Seth. Were the committing acts of sodomy, incest and beastiality.

Whereas; they intermingled with southern continents prior to the establishment of any form of religious, political, educational and spiritual foundation being organized and ordained into shaping factors form humankind.

Therefore; the K'un is also misunderstood as bonding factors of uniting. However: it is true to an extent. Meaning, this is to the extent of the inducement of negative traits / behavioral patterns that includes excessive pleasures to the modificational factors towards likes and dislikes. Therefore: Beware of personal favortism. For this is written in the second chapter of James in the Holy Bible as well as the Ka Region of the Kamitic Tree of Life as it relates to The Zero Dynastic ProtoDynastic and PreDynastic Periods of Egypt.

These behaviors of excessiveness are the results of neurological— neurocognitive dyfunctions through pathogens of DNA and RNA strand development within an individuals genome index or genetic inprint. In this, stimuli can be directly a true and divne guide or it can be directly / indirectly forms of misguiding factors in the shaping factors of the manipulation processes of the use of the will.

The will is internal. However; i must be externally {willed} carried out with true and devoted compassion of proceeding to manifest the [Blessing] that one have e mindful with proper guidance of GODS TRUE WISDOM. Also, RAPID PROGRESS—Hexagram #35 CHIN—mentions "Not Just Simply A Counsel"

Therefore, there's no need for details. Needless to say, "Leave The details to True God! By seeing the whole at its entirety, there will be less disappointment in the end. You'll be assurred that wisdom will always welcome inner-peace with the understanding that details are for uses of survival. This therefore, has negative effects on the adrenal glands and the entire nervous system.

You see, in modifying negative emotional and behavioral patterns, individuals must have knowledge of the entire spectrum. This inludes the following;

1. Neuropathological Disorder
2. Neuromuscular Disorder
3. The Entire Nervous System
4. The Spiritual Practice of which he or she is practicing
5. The scope of the Anatomical Process
6.

The entire origin of culture, race, religion, anatomy of sexes, and the effects of their total variations in the form of response to direct and indirect forms of stimuli. This is to say— "let wisdom speak for itself— instead of pseudo-intellectualitis forms of rheteric".

K'un is a combination Heru, Het Heru and Auset, Nekhebet and Uatchet. They can be detrimental towards others. Especially, those who are of the lower being of the Ka Region.

TRUE CORRECTIVENESS COMES FROM GOD WITHIN

True correctiveness is absorbed and comes from the God within every living organism. However: There is only one True and superior Creator who is the Divine God of all existing beings whom are seeking divinity. The one creator who has provided Shepherds, Theologeons, Priests, Teachers and Scribes to guide and provide His True instruction unto the multitudes. The multitudes include the lowly and those who are at the lower-being spiritually. This includes those with neuropsychiatric, degenerative disorders and dysfunctions with regards to inconsistancies within their realm of the lack spiritual knowledge and thinking therof.

Therefore: whom has the mind of the True God that he might instruct Him. Was it not pleasing to the True God, The True Creator to teach those who believed that He Is The True God and True Creator of The Universe for more than trillions of years prior to those words being inscribed on papers—scrolls and carved on stones of heiroglyphic design.

You see, the I-Ching Hexagram #4 Ming = Youthful Folly— relates to adrenal disorders of the limbic system, mammilian cortex and hippocampus. Whereas: Receptors are proteins that reside within and on the membrains of postysynaptic neuron(s). In addition, neurotransmitters

GABA deal with the entire nervous system is it relates to the cerebral spinal index and enhances psychiatric stimulated chemicals that triggers forms of behavioral and educational patterns within the ovaries and fetus—eventually grows within each child throughout his her stages of total development.

Romans 2:21 you who teach others—do you not teach yourselves. You teach others but fail to live whatever your teachings are. You boast about the law and the laws of God— however; you do not live them or it.

Therefore: true correctiveness from The True God. True correctiveness is then passed on like a degenerative pathogen.

This can be dealth with either truthfully or untruthfully. As a result, you have fooled and harmed others by destroying their lives with youthful folliness as well as the fooling of ones self.

However: impart wisdom by not sparing the rod upon anyone who needs the guidance of Gods discipline. However: in Proverbs 13:24 it says "Whoever spares the rod hates their children, but whoever loves their children will discipline them with sound forms of disciple that incorporates obedience".

In this: the pathological affects will be great. Whereas: the children will not be victims of child abuse and neglect as well as the shaken baby syndrome. This is an important mantra for everyone. The children will not have to become involved within the state department of child protective services and so on.

Also, the adult(s) will not be involved within the department of corrections. This includes the prison system or psychiatric institution having to deal and cope with conditions concerning nerological disorders that includes degeneratives.

Moving right along: in Surah 20:115-116 it is written as follows:

And certainly—We gave a commandment to Adam before, but he forgot: and We found in Him no Resolve (to disobey) and when We said to the angels: Be submissive to Adam, they submitted except Iblis, he refused. Therefore, it was no intention for Adam to disobey. However: the counsel of the angel—deity—shepherd disobeyed.

Youn see, in Jeremiah 23—it discussess situations regarding false shepherds and leaders of all ranks and religions who are scattering the sheep of Gods pasture. Therefore: this is a the incorrect use of the WILL. This also include false forms of correctiveness that is being taught unto the lowly as well as poor leadership by individuals who are in positions of employed authority.

For they are followers of the inventions of evil things. Romans 1:30 Slanderers, God haters, insolent, arrogant and boastful.

They invent ways of doing evil through Transgenic Organisms, Genetic Inprinting, DNA Methylation and Genomic DNA infrastructuring in order of creating and producing congenital abnormalities. Abnormalities include disorders that are too disgusting to address in this particular book!

Finally, Behavioral correctiveness is a lifelong journey. It begins with humility but not losing one's values of self- reliance. It means that God's true essence shall shine upon the just. It also means that you are not certified as becoming victims of the ungodly and unjust. Keep your eye open by seeing the whole. In addition: you must realize that wisdom is an understanding that excessive passions of profane and vile forms of gene promotion shouldn't occur. Especially on the bases of [repressiveness] and effortless methods of sharing, giving and providing whatever is crucial in the positive reenforcement within the enhancement of a people and individuals. Whether it be of culture or tribunal union.

CHAPTER 7

MAGNETIC FIELDS

ANCESTOR DEFICIT DISORDER

Luke 11:47 Woe to you, because you build tombs for the prophets, and it was your ancestors who killed them. In addition: I Corinthians 15:56 The sting of death is sin. For the sting is like a gene gun. Death is like a neurodegenerative disorder that murders the entire nervous system. However: it says that power over sin is the divine principles within all of the Laws of The True God beyond the Zero Dynasty. THEREFORE; SURAH 17:11 EVERY DEED DOES HAS A CONSEQUENCE. In addition in Surah 17:75 "Then We would have made thee taste a double punishment in life and a double punishment after death and thou wouldst not have a helper against us".

THIS BOOK WAS WRITTEN BY:

Rev. Dr. Aneb Jah Rasta Sensas-Utcha Nefer-1 DD Owner: Tejauma Na Nia Corp. Milwaukee, Wisconsin

www.ingramcontent.com/pod-product-compliance
Lightning Source LLC
Chambersburg PA
CBHW030546290526
45786CB00004B/1886